EMBRACING
NATURAL
DESIGN

EMBRACING NATURAL DESIGN

Inspired Living

Stephanie Kienle Gonzalez

FOREWORD BY INDIA HICKS

RIZZOLI NEW YORK

New York · Paris · London · Milan

For Chris, Andrea, Arielle, and Anouck.
Home is wherever you are.

CONTENTS

FOREWORD

David and I embraced under-decorating long ago, and now here is Stephanie taking the ideas of organic forms and natural materials to insane levels of dreaminess, inspiring us all to create the most exquisite, perfect spaces that no one ever wants to leave.

Stephanie feels like such a kindred spirit to me. We share a fondness for palm fronds and the responsibility of decorating being the family business. Having spent nomadic youths studying and adventuring around the globe led us both to devote a good chunk of our time as adults to creating homes for our families. These are places to display the odd treasure or two found while traveling, but they are not museums by any stretch of the imagination. Instead, our homes serve as soft landing spots for our own tribes along with an ever-rotating group of interesting people and their entertaining stories.

Stephanie makes me believe in the possibilities of the future. From her commitment to supporting Filipino craftspeople to her gentle nudges toward an environmentally conscious lifestyle, Stephanie shows us what to do next.

Surely, her two beautiful daughters, and a third one on her way, are the main reasons for her devotion to a beautiful future for all. We must learn all we can from Stephanie to make sure there are palm trees and rhinos for the next generations to see. Thank goodness for this exquisite woman living a life of style with a conscience.

—India Hicks

INTRODUCTION

The house was in the middle of the Serengeti. It had been restored and was now a bright and airy space and, as I entered, I felt as though I could glide from one room to another, delighting in the magnificent landscape peeking through the windows. That view took my breath away.

It was December 2012, and we were on a family holiday. The house may have been 6,000 miles from Manila, where I live, but I felt right at home. The interior was warm, natural, and tactile—a cocoon of well-designed comfort. I remember this house and the emotions it evoked with such fondness that, to this day, it comes to mind whenever I approach a new design project. I hope that I am able to express myself just as clearly and inspire similar feelings in my clients, family, and friends, igniting a desire to live consciously, joyfully, and with great purpose.

I've visited many remarkable places throughout my life, from lush tropical villas in Southeast Asia to Parisian apartments that have been restored to full modernity, and even striking traditional African homesteads where heritage has left its indelible stamp. While I appreciate a wide range of styles, those that resonate with me have a natural charm and personality of their own. Many of the spaces I have come to love aren't particularly "perfect" in terms of design but have an authenticity that reflects the homeowner's character and life. The thoughtful layering of these spaces, a harmonious blend of form, function, and sentiment, gives meaning to the space.

Throughout the pages of this book, I share the personal spaces in which I have spent hours passionately working, entertaining, and relaxing. Each design experience imparts an invaluable lesson in intuition, exploration, collaboration, and creativity. I relish the opportunity to share with you the spaces I call home and the craft I am passionate about. As you join me on this visual journey, I encourage you to let the intimate stories, actionable ideas, awareness of nature, and designers who have influenced me, breathe life into your own endeavors.

OPPOSITE: A family trip to the Grumeti Reserve, Tanzania, in 2012. Singita's Serengeti House's covered terrace inspired me as it frames the majestic scenery filled with wildlife. It has had a lasting impact on me.

10

My Inspirations

THE PEOPLE IN MY LIFE

More than simply being a unique appearance or a distinctive form of expression, style comes from the people, places, and experiences that inspire us every day. My mother, Zelda, epitomizes finesse and grace—quite the opposite of my clumsy, rough-around-the-edges childhood self. She is simply beautiful. She always reminds me that less is more and that I can never go wrong with "classic." While most women her age pile on makeup and jewelry, Mom has stayed true to herself and has instead shed layers. Nowadays, she is most comfortable in a white polo and jeans. Her taste in interiors is similarly understated, her bright home a picture of tradition and subdued elegance throughout. Hers is a calming, monochromatic palette, with soft white textures from floor to ceiling and pockets of greenery here and there, along with refined decor and meaningful objects.

My mom's mother, Lola Monina, has been a nurturing force in my life. Raising nine children is a feat in itself and my Lola did it effortlessly, nourishing everyone literally and figuratively with her outstandingly delicious food, such as my favorites, beef *mechado* and chicken adobo, a much-loved dish in the Kienle household. I would like to think that she has passed on to my mom, who in turn passed on to me, a love of welcoming people into your home and the desire to nurture guests.

I would call very few people iconic, but Edith Neyrinck Kienle would certainly make the cut. My grandmother was a wonderfully kind, classically beautiful lady, slender and perennially tanned, with an untamable energy and spirit. Born to Belgian parents in Antwerp in 1924, who then moved the family to the Congo, she spent half her life in the lush African wilderness and the other half in picture-perfect Lausanne, Switzerland. Grany, "La Star," is one of my biggest inspirations. Although she appreciated life's luxuries, she enjoyed them sparingly. Grany knew how to do things "just right"; she was never over the top, but never underwhelming, either. She taught me that refinement requires restraint, so that you can focus on what matters.

Grany's life on the vast and captivating African continent intrigued me the most about her. After marrying my grandfather Albert, twenty-five years her senior, in the 1940s, her life became an "Out of Africa" adventure—wild and romantic. I spent countless hours listening as she relived her memories, her descriptions so vivid it was difficult to believe the events had occurred half a century ago. My father, Max, who spent his youth in the Congo, would chime in as she recounted these tales, saying, "While you go to the mall on the weekends in Manila, my childhood days were spent exploring the wild with our jeep, picnic and rifle in tow, searching for all kinds of adventure." It was my Grany and

OPPOSITE, CLOCKWISE FROM TOP: My mother exploring the idyllic Boracay Island in the Philippines in the early 1980s with her then boyfriend, my dad, Max. They stayed in rustic *bahay kubos*, or nipa huts, without electricity. The huts—made of bamboo and cogon grass—were surrounded by lush coconut forests. My mother with her dog Chino soon after my parent's marriage in the garden of their first furniture workshop in Manila. My grandfather, Lolo Daning, fishing in Palawan in the Philippines. He was an adventurer with a great love of nature.

my dad who ignited my interest and love of travel, and their African roots form an intrinsic part of my identity.

When I became a mom, I started to see things differently. Although I have always been a sentimental person, my perspective shifted, so that the meaning behind every event or item became even more important. Every decision about the design of our family home was made with my daughters in mind. My husband, Chris, and I may have vowed that we wouldn't change our lifestyle when they came into our lives, but our home certainly reflects their presence—the pen marks on the furniture, the tiny handprints on our windows, and the odd stuffed toy buried under our throw pillows. This makes our home all the more special to me, as their playfulness inspires me every day.

FAMILY ROOTS

My father, Max, a Swiss national, was born in the now Democratic Republic of the Congo. After he met my mom in Manila, where he was living, he decided to leave his corporate job and try his luck on his own in the Philippines, then called the "Pearl of the Orient." His decision to stay laid the foundation for our Filipino Swiss family.

My sister and I, both born and raised in Manila, have spent our lives shifting between European and Asian cultures because of family ties and close friends. My affinity for Africa was born out of my father's childhood stories and has grown in recent years as I continue to explore the continent with my husband and children.

However, when I think of home, it's the Philippines that comes to mind. The capital, Manila, a chaotic concrete jungle, has become more cosmopolitan over the years: the country's over 7,000 islands are the epitome of a beach lover's paradise—coconut trees swaying against a vast blue sky, pristine waters, powdery white sand, a richly textured and mesmerizingly colorful marine life, and that world-famous Filipino smile. Although we currently live in a tall building in an urban hub, these magnificent escapes are never more than a short drive or flight away and, because of that, tropical living is very much a part of our lifestyle.

OPPOSITE, CLOCKWISE FROM TOP LEFT: My grandparents, Edith and Albert, on one of their monthlong sea voyages from the Congo to Europe. Always chic, Grany was never without her pearl necklace and a long brown menthol cigarette between her fingers. My father, Max, boating on the Lualaba River. As a young boy, he was always on the lookout for hippopotamuses and the next grand animal sighting. Grany with her children, Max and Anne, exploring the bush around Likasi, in the Haut-Katanga Province of the Democratic Republic of the Congo. Grany in her youth in Europe.

LEFT: Grany Edith and her children, Max and Anne, photographed in the Democratic Republic of the Congo in the 1950s by my grandfather, Albert, who loved the latest gadgets of the time and was an avid photographer.

PAGE 18: The beauty of the Philippine islands—here, *bangkas*, or traditional outrigger boats, are surrounded by the pristine waters of the mountainous island Coron.

PAGE 19: On safari in Tswalu Kalahari Game Reserve, South Africa, with my girls, Andrea and Arielle.

RIGHT: Striking El Nido with its famous steep limestone cliffs and swaying coconut trees, in Palawan in the Philippines.

DESIGN VIEWPOINT

FROM DREAM TO DESIGN

I t all starts with a dream. Whenever I am presented with the prospect of creating a space, I feel invigorated, my excitement barely contained and my ideas start to flow. I fully enjoy this process: being able to start with a blank canvas and conceptualize the shapes, colors, and textures—endless possibilities.

I find designing a home to be an incredibly creative and tantalizing process, pulling together the skills of many people to help shape your vision and bring it to reality. Because a home is a sacred, personal space that grows and evolves with your life story, it is an extension of your identity, where you can be your truest self, where you feel at peace—inspired and surrounded by the things and people you love.

When I envisaged our completed homes, I imagined them as stylishly charming, functional, and filled with sentimental possessions—treasured artwork, furniture I partly designed, hand-me-down pieces, artifacts from family travels, and the odd kiddie items. Objects tie your look together, the small details that make your space original and authentic. Treasured possessions remind me of the twists and turns of our family journey. I love the idea of creating a home for inspiration and not as a showcase. The elements in it should move you, and convey aspects of your life, personality, and individuality. Fill your space with a mix of simple and notable pieces that you want to pass from one generation to the next.

When I am asked "what's your style?" I can never give a simple answer, because my style evolves as my life and experiences do. My design sensibility transforms as I discover new artisans and artists who resonate with me. People love to categorize and apply labels to interior design, and while I understand the need to do so, I have never felt obliged to adhere to a particular look. I feel that *eclectic* has become an overused word that describes a combination of styles, but it defines best how I enjoy mixing textures and elements from different time periods—a modern take on traditional styles that includes natural elements.

I honor and admire tradition, but when it comes to design, I enjoy giving the traditional a contemporary twist. I try to create a visual oxymoron, juxtaposing old and new, classic and contemporary, masculine and feminine, patina and polish. Unexpected combinations energize me, allowing me to fashion evocative spaces that resonate with their surroundings.

The wooden pieces in my home are a reflection of this. Wood is a material you find in many houses in the Philippines, and I love having

PAGE 22: One focal point of our living room is a Philux Luna sofa, upholstered in a textured cream linen. A Serge Mouille light fixture in black adds a modern sculptural touch.

PAGE 23: A close-up of one of the lush staghorns that hangs on our terrace column.

OPPOSITE: A play on textural contrasts: A sleek Philux custom bar cabinet with shagreen paneling with a Fernando Zóbel de Ayala y Montojo framed print titled *El Jardín* hung above it. The purchase of this print initiated our Filipino art collection. A warthog skull sits atop the cabinet with carved giraffe sculptures from South Africa on the floor.

pieces that continue this tradition while also bringing nature's warmth and tactility into my home. All our pieces are made from wood that has been grown sustainably—a modern statement against the loss of hardwood forests.

I also like to reference our distinctive culture through textiles. We are fortunate to manufacture interesting fabrics in the Philippines. These materials aren't just prized for their beauty—many community projects have been developed around these fabrics, making them a symbol of hope and empowerment as well. Blending these cultural icons with the hallmarks of other traditions and countries allows me to express the many facets of our lifestyle and culture.

Bringing in Nature

Mother Nature is one of the best artists. An unpolished stone surface invites you to reach out and touch it, hammered metal imbues a sense of earthiness, and seagrass wallpaper adds a touch of coziness. I have always felt nourished by nature, even as a child, as I grew up hearing stories of my father's childhood in the jungles of the Congo and, later, saw how my mother transformed our city apartment into a home by making it a haven for greenery—potted plants, orchids, giant palms, and small bonsai arrangements.

Nature helps us connect with our senses, and natural light and greenery add life, vibrance, and serenity to your space. It has been so important to me to incorporate nature's essential elements in our residences, especially in Manila, where we are surrounded by concrete. Our terrace has become a peaceful oasis amid a bustling city, where staghorns, bougainvillea, ficus trees, potted plants, and succulents meet. Finding ways to bring nature, inherently therapeutic and meditative, closer to you will not only beautify your personal space but also create an atmosphere of genuine happiness.

One way of doing this is by filling a vase with fresh flowers—one of my greatest pleasures. They bring life to any room and provide an extra dimension to decor. Orchids are a favorite, with their sculptural shapes and spectrum of colors and patterns. They fit into any room, subtly confident and beautiful, adding sensuality to a space. They also last longer than many other floral varieties and are fairly low maintenance. I make a point of keeping the plants after the blooms have faded and repotting them in our office garden.

OPPOSITE: King proteas in a clear vase. Choosing a simple and sleek vessel allows nature's bounty to take center stage.

FOLLOWING SPREAD: Over thirty floors above street level, this pocket terrace is our urban outdoor refuge, replete with lush greenery, Philux furniture, and *Bamileke* coffee tables from Africa. I created an orchid "tree" using cemented driftwood in pottery as a base; I replenish it with different orchid varieties.

Conscious Living

I find the idea of making choices that don't suit just me but can also help local communities and have a soft impact on the environment incredibly appealing. This can be something as simple as choosing a piece made locally, by an artisan whose skills have become part of the object's story. Or, using your creativity to find a second life for a piece of furniture you have loved, or even just selecting the very best quality you can find so that an item will give you many years of pleasure.

Art in Your Home

Soon after Chris and I married and moved into our home, we developed an interest in art. We realized we would have to find a way to decorate the walls of the long, narrow entrance hall in our new apartment. We both had an appreciation for design in general and shared a similar aesthetic, although his tastes lean toward the modern while mine skew more traditional.

Putting our first home together proved exciting and tedious in equal measure, as we balanced our dreams, budget, and sensibilities. As our first investment we purchased a Fernando Zóbel de Ayala y Montojo print in 2010. While it is modest in size, we hung it with pride in our bedroom, where it has brought us a lot of joy. We have taken immense pleasure in building our collection. At the outset, we didn't know very much, but we made an effort to learn about local art and searched for pieces from renowned Filipino artists that we believed to offer good value. Our burgeoning love of art flourished during our South African honeymoon, where we came to love the country's aesthetic. It made sense to us to not only collect art that was African in origin but to embrace this as a theme for our small yet growing collection.

Since then, we have come to place less emphasis on the provenance of a piece and have adopted a more intuitive approach to art. We typically favor compositions depicting an aspect of Africa—whether wildlife photography, antique bronze sculptures, or ornate carved wooden masks. All of these diverse pieces come together beautifully in our rooms, and the subtle underlying story that links them makes our collection all the more special. I like adding a sculptural element to every room, playing with different mediums and scales to create depth and bring in a touch of the unexpected.

OPPOSITE: An oil painting from BenCab's *Sabel* series hangs beside a bronze cheetah by Dylan Lewis. The Boston fern, housed in a woven vintage pot, enlivens the artwork.

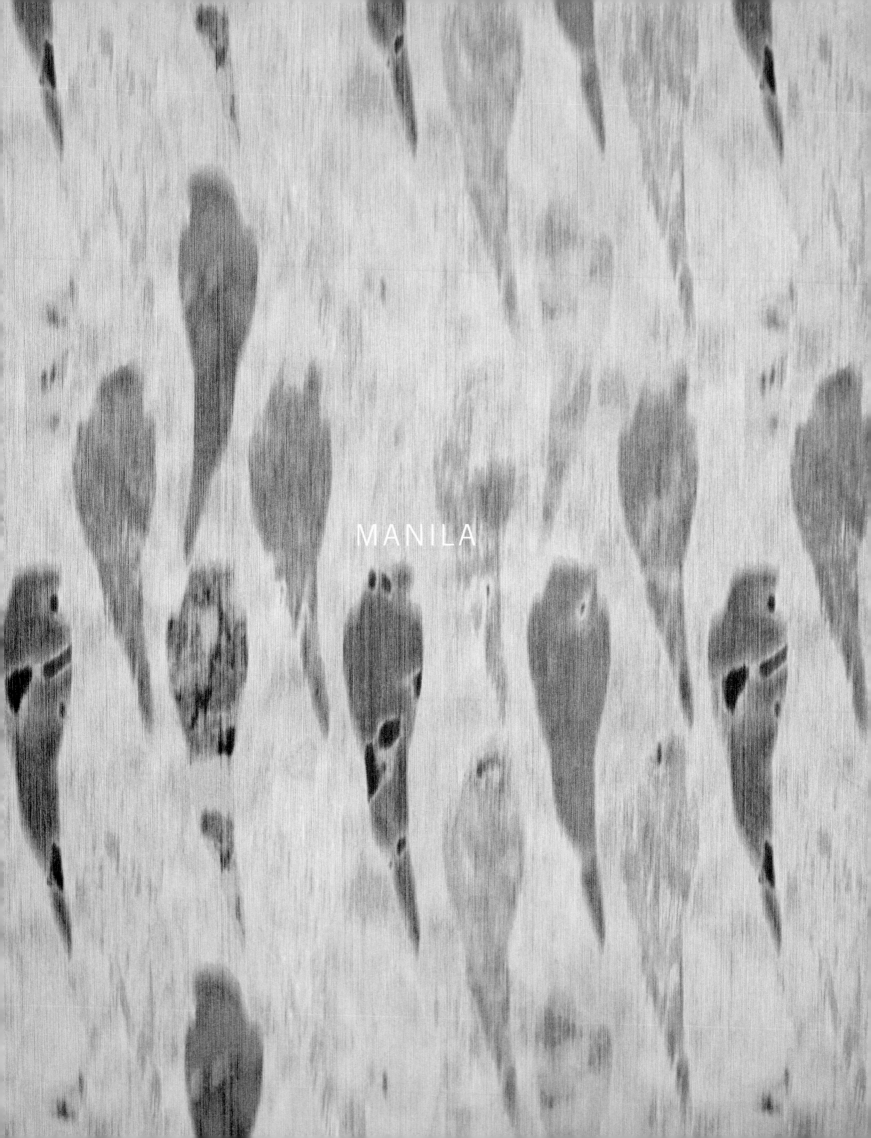

MANILA

A GRACIOUS APARTMENT

PAGE 32: A traditional Filipino
kalesa, or horse-drawn
carriage, in Fort Santiago,
Intramuros, Manila.

PAGE 33: Painterly Arte Manakin
Maringa wallpaper in our den
camouflages sliding pocket doors
that conceal a television—a clever
design to keep technology from
intruding in an open-plan space.

OPPOSITE: Lionel Smit's large
portrait hung in the double-
height living room informed
the space's color palette. The
rug, which I codesigned with
Iñigo Elizalde, was inspired by
a hybrid of leopard rosettes
and feathers in the same
muted tones as the oil painting.
Filling the opposite wall,
Olivia d'Aboville's handwoven
Philippine silk artwork represents
the great migration of wildlife
moving toward greener pastures.
Paint, stones, and beadwork
embellish the sofa's throw pillows
by Bea Valdes Design.

Having grown up in a bustling city, I have always been partial to apartment living. The convenience of location, maintenance, and facilities is a big advantage, and in my case, having my parents in the same building has really added to a sense of ease and comfort. We live in a family-friendly residential neighborhood with pockets of green space, cafés, and shops. Returning here after living in another frantic part of Manila felt like returning to my childhood home, but this time with the option of designing a space to fit my every whim. I fell in love all over again with the generous, bright space of the apartment and the quietly splendid pocket terrace—a lush green escape separating the living and dining areas. This was the canvas on which I would cultivate a home that made us feel nurtured and inspired.

The building was about fifteen years old and the place needed a full revamp because we wanted to upgrade many of the integral parts such as plumbing, air-conditioning, and lighting for longevity. Additionally, we wanted to develop a thoughtful architectural design that fit our current lifestyle and would allow for our growing family to evolve without further construction. In other words, we went for a one-time, big-time renovation that required a significant investment of both time and resources—as well as our full attention.

For this project, we worked with architect Alfred Wieneke—he helped us put together a clean slate by reengineering the staircase and hiding exposed ceiling beams found throughout the unit. Interior designer Isabel Lozano helped with interiors and sourcing, while Mark Wilson and Nikki Tayag of Wilson Escalona Design participated in putting together a cohesive lighting concept that addressed the needs of the existing architecture. Generally speaking, I find myself decisive with the direction I want to explore in interiors, and I thrive in collaborations to get the most out of the design experience. Having a creative soundboard always brings a fresh and exciting perspective to any project.

The Look and Feel

Living in the tropics, I feel strongly about choosing the right materials for furniture and decor. I try to opt for those that fit the spirit of the place, but I do not hesitate to add my personal touch to keep things as authentic as possible. A mix of Asian, European, and African sensibilities greets you; the apartment is an ode to a subtle combination of simple, yet luxurious, natural materials, layered with texture upon texture of neutral tones.

The memories from our current Manila apartment fills me with nostalgia—many a fun evening with friends and music on our terrace, daylight dance parties with my girls in the den, family cookouts shared around our oval dining table, and peaceful mornings to meditate with our Yorkshire terrier, Clooney, by my side, as I sip a cup of tea.

We surround ourselves with such basic and notable objects, such as "woodbird," a driftwood sculpture from a Zimbabwean artist, a hand-sculpted bronze vessel from Lamont, and an antique Tang dynasty horse, each depicting in its own way with form, function, and sentiment. Some we have purchased because of their beauty and practicality; others have an aesthetic quality and a meaningful story behind them. Layering these elements brings warmth to any space.

OPPOSITE: A tree trunk table that sits on a patchwork rug from ABC Carpet in New York anchors the foyer. The table's glass top allows the tree roots to be appreciated from all angles. An antique Chinese Song dynasty (early tenth century) jar excavated from the Mindanao Lanao del Norte Province in the Philippines is filled with green *Salix*, or curly willow, branches. The staircase is clad in oak veneer.

FOLLOWING SPREAD: The bright living room is furnished with the Pacific buffet in walnut by Philux, a Serge Mouille light fixture, and a custom marble coffee table. Touches of greenery bring nature in, and the antiques and curios on display provide a patina and soul to the space.

36

OPPOSITE: The Love Handles ceramic vase by Anissa Kermiche adds a playful touch and contrast to the airy palette of the room.

RIGHT: I display colorful plates by artist Ruan Hoffmann on the living room's coffee table and built-in oak shelf. Chris and I purchased them during our honeymoon in Cape Town, South Africa, from a gallery in the Stellenbosch Winelands.

BELOW: A driftwood sculpture dubbed "woodbird" by a Zimbabwean artisan is one of my favorite travel finds.

FOLLOWING SPREAD: The custom dining room table is a repurposed piece that has had several iterations as we changed our living locations—it first had a rectangular glass top, then a solid walnut top, and now an oval-shaped travertine. Philux's Embla and Polk chairs, upholstered in velvet, flank the table. Lindsey Adelman's branching bubble light fixture hangs above it. Kelly Wearstler's Trancas credenza sits under the Fernando Zóbel de Ayala y Montojo oil painting and solid rock-crystal sconces by Phoenix Gallery, New York.

PAGE 44: In the den, a Milo Baughman brass and upholstered lounge chair and ottoman from Restoration Hardware sit adjacent to a petrified wood stump from Indonesia. Displayed on the built-in shelves is a Hernando Ruiz Ocampo painting, which provides a backdrop for a Ramon Orlina glass sculpture. An antique bust from Cambodia graces another shelf.

PAGE 45: Mario Bellini's Camaleonda sofa in moss green anchors the den and delivers a pop of color.

OPPOSITE, CLOCKWISE FROM TOP LEFT: A detail of the Mario Bellini sofa showing its bulbous design. A custom chandelier by Diego Mardegan for Glustin Luminaries adds sculptural volume and light to the room. It is made of brass and parchment paper shades. The feather Duck Feet lamp by Porta Romana is one of my favorite pieces. The soft and metallic elements make it wonderfully tactile. A custom bench by Philux, upholstered in Pierre Frey leopard velvet.

ABOVE: The stylish custom rattan commode by E. Murio is a functional piece that houses my table linens. Hanging above it is a painting by renowned Filipino master Fernando Amorsolo, who is known for his landscapes.

PREVIOUS SPREAD: For the main bedroom, Philux's Stockholm bed in solid, sustainably sourced ash is flanked by the company's Oslo night tables with abaca matting and the Valencia upholstered bench. These pieces from Philux's Scandiniana collection reflect Scandinavian mid-century design with reference to Filipino artisanship. The modern shapes are warmed up by the natural Filipino textures of *solihiya*, or cane and abaca weaves.

OPPOSITE: A quiet reading nook is furnished with a modern B&B Italia chair with a linen slipcover, a sculpture by Armenian artist Nina Khemchyan, and an antique Burmese drum, used as a side table.

RIGHT: A mirrored metal desk and Philux Polk chair add sophistication to the bedroom.

PAGE 52: The animal prints provide a touch of whimsy to the nursery. The white frames and soft cream Filipino textiles supply calming accents to the black-and-white Thibaut Panthera wallpaper.

PAGE 53: A peacock chair from South Africa is paired with a whitewashed wooden stump side table and a modern black standing lamp. The hand-carved standing mirror was custom made in the Philippines.

LEFT: Art that is close to my heart: My young daughter Andrea showed an interest in the artworks hanging on the walls of our home, so my husband and I have included her in our discussions about artists. When Andrea started to paint, she worried about scribbling outside the lines until I encouraged her to express what she feels. We display both of our daughters' creations throughout our home. Here in the playroom, their framed artwork mingles with their Lego constructions of fanciful rooms and buildings.

PAGE 56: Andrea's room is the epitome of a little girl's pink dream. Classic white moldings, a textured blush wallpaper, and playful frames dress up one wall. Her Philux Little Copen desk in sustainable ash is paired with a Little Tana chair upholstered in a rich pink velvet with nail-head accents.

PAGE 57: When our daughters decided to share a room, they requested that I design a bunk bed for them. The Philux team came up with this simple design that includes cane detailing and woven storage baskets below. Now the girls have expanded play space.

LAPALALA

A FAMILY RETREAT IN SOUTH AFRICA

PAGE 58: The terrace is a lovely spot to enjoy the outdoors. Rustic wicker armchairs from Cebu in the Philippines surround a *riempie* coffee table from South Africa.

PAGE 59: Seen from the firepit, a close-up of the sandstone cladding of the house with hanging carved wooden Giriama posts from Kenya.

PREVIOUS SPREAD: This striking rock facade is located within the northern border of the Lapalala Reserve, where the Kgokong and Palala Rivers meet at Tambouti.

OPPOSITE: As the sun slowly rises behind the mystical rock cliff, the trees surrounding the Lapalala property glisten and the grass dampened by morning dew sparkles—this is my favorite time of the day. It is an ideal moment to quietly observe the sights and sounds as the bush comes to life, while I sip my first cup of tea under the arbor.

ittle can rival Africa's golden hour. As the sun sets, a spectacular warm glaze gives the rugged landscape a glow. From my favorite spot at my Lapalala home, fondly called the Modumela House, which refers to a white syringa tree found around the property, I can see the majestic cliffs come to life as the rays paint them a bright burnt orange. The shouts of a rowdy troop of baboons echo off the rock, bouncing over the river. I sit still and absorb the splendor. Something about this moment makes me feel small—Africa's natural beauty is humbling. It makes me pause and appreciate the simple, honest things nature has to offer. Africa is the only place I experience such stillness and, simultaneously, an outpouring of life.

With its primordial wilderness and sprawling, dramatic landscape set against a blazing South African sky, Lapalala feels like heaven on earth. We stumbled upon this beautiful nature reserve in 2015, and it made me fall in love with South Africa all over again. My husband echoed this sentiment; we took a leap of faith together when we decided to make it a home for our family.

Conscious Conservation

Lapalala, located in the abundant Waterberg habitat, is "a treasure house of biological . . . cultural, geological, and archaeological diversity," as naturalist and artist Clive Walker, one of the reserve's founders, writes in his book *Lapalala Wilderness*. We were immediately drawn to this conservation project, which saw Walker and cofounder South African conservationist Dale Parker rehabilitate 50,000 hectares of farmland to its wild natural state in 1981.

In its latest iteration, the reserve is managed by a board of like-minded conservationists led by Duncan Parker and Gianni Ravazzotti, for whom sustainability forms a core value. Under their guidance, Lapalala Reserve's sustainability program includes community projects and several scientific endeavors, such as a special-species breeding center and a cheetah research program. Additionally, the Lapalala Wilderness School, which has served over 70,000 children, aims to nurture and develop the biodiversity of the area and to champion future conservationists across Africa.

Our involvement as custodians of this incredible place is not limited to enjoying what it offers visitors but extends to supporting the mission of protecting and maintaining nature's balance here. Advocating a green lifestyle for our children has always been a central tenet of our parenting,

and this project has brought much joy and purpose to our family. We are grateful to be a part of this slice of wilderness, and we hope to share this nature preservation experience and mindset with others.

The pleasure of being in a pristine environment—away from the plastic, pollution, and clamor—has become a real luxury to me. These days, luxury is about how you manage your time, synonymous with the freedom that comes from being able to disconnect from the noise of our quotidian lives and find tranquility in nature. When I get away from the deluge of thoughts and distractions of my daily life, I find inner peace, and I have come to savor this simplicity—stripping away the unessential and finding deep fulfillment in an elementary state where life slows down.

Modumela House Design: Blending Tradition with Contemporary Natural Style

When we discovered the Modumela site, we knew it was where we wanted to build our home away from home. Nestled in the middle of the reserve, its vistas encompass a striking rock cliff, the Palala River, a mountain view, and an overgrown green plain. A 1922 Ransomes, Sims & Jefferies steam engine sits, a hulking historical relic, near the riverbed. Walking away from the meandering river one day, I spotted a modest fig tree and convinced Chris to make this the center of our garden. Today, it has grown handsomely and watches over the inviting water hole that brings a surprising abundance of wildlife close to our home.

Modumela House blends unobtrusively into the beautiful landscape with as little impact on the environment as possible. It was built completely off the grid, using solar energy as the main source of power and incorporating other green elements, such as rain catchment containers and an evaporative cooling system. The small roof garden above the kitchen is my favorite architectural feature, allowing the house to meld into the rocky hill that serves as its geological mold.

We built the two-story family house in red stone we excavated from the hill on the property; we wanted to use as many local materials as possible—including the stonework, the slasto, or slate, pavement, and the reed ceilings and joinery. Our floors are a domestic rendition of classic terrazzo—again, consisting of a mixture of aggregate chips of stone from the area and concrete. We used large glass panes throughout the house to bring light in and disappearing sliding doors in the common areas to accentuate the connection to the surrounding natural landscape. The terraces open up to a spacious lawn, a pool, and two guest suites tucked away from the main house for a sense of privacy in the bush.

PREVIOUS SPREAD: The ancient rock facade and river was the first place we visited in the Lapalala Reserve in South Africa in 2015. Near this powerful natural wonder is where we decided to build our home so that we can enjoy the view and sounds up close.

OPPOSITE: Every vignette in the home is an opportunity to share our family story. The map of Africa is from my husband Chris's vintage map collection. On the hand-forged iron console by Trevor Opperman stand two expressive wooden masks purchased during a trip to Tanzania. Next to them is a treasured photograph from the first time my parents and my sister's family visited Modumela House.

The interiors draw inspiration from Africa's traditional homestead, a design we modernized and made more personal. We blended European and local aesthetics, and added a touch of Filipino culture, notably in the woven furniture, such as our dining and accent chairs. I also included Victorian spotted bamboo tables. The textiles are a mix of African and European with contrasting raw textures, *Shweshwe* fabrics (bright colored with intricate geometrical patterns), and more delicate block prints. I covered a traditional European chandelier with raffia shades to give it interesting contrast and natural flair. You will find shells from the Philippines, antique prints of Madagascar and the Manila port, and a wide variety of tokens representing our family's diverse roots.

We engaged architect Julia Williams and interior designer Yvonne O'Brien to help realize our vision. Working with them on this remote home construction presented a novel challenge, but collaborating on a transcontinental project proved exciting and stimulating. Our house was designed for the comfort and joy that family life brings. As much as I love tradition, I do not want our homes to feel stuck in a decorative time warp but rather to reflect some old, some new, and some unexpected and charming accents that resonate with us.

The overall look is tactile and thoughtfully layered—a thread that weaves throughout the house—and meant to make our guests feel truly at home, free to kick up their feet, unwind, and bask in peaceful, natural comfort. Each detail reflects who we are, imbuing our home with an energy, spirit, and stories we gratefully share.

OPPOSITE: A pair of classic wooden curio cabinets, lined with seagrass, in the living room. On display are books and objects d'art.

PAGE 70: Transitional spaces are great for design moments. This hallway leading to the bedrooms is clad with natural sandstone on one side and has floor-to-ceiling glass on the other, allowing for natural light and the outdoor environment to be integrated with the indoors. It also functions as a gallery of Chris's wildlife photographs taken during our travels throughout Africa.

PAGE 71: Our sunken deck is a space we enjoy midday and, in the evenings, when we huddle around a fire and recount the day's activities and animal sightings.

PREVIOUS SPREAD AND
OPPOSITE: Timeworn materials
give the sitting room character.
The two large Belgian-style
upholstered sofas, flanked by
Philippine-made armchairs
woven in jute rope, surround
a chocolate leather trunk and
a contemporary stone-top
metal coffee table, which have
been placed side by side. A
vintage crystal chandelier hangs
above, infusing the room with
traditional elegance.

ABOVE RIGHT: On our terrace,
a round table covered in a
Hessian textured cloth is
surrounded by rattan-framed
chairs with *lampacanay* strips
and rope binding from Cebu in
the Philippines.

FOLLOWING SPREAD:
The Directoire desk in
sustainable walnut, a classic
Philux design, faces a hand-
painted mural by Tessa Metcalf—
an ode to the beauty of the
surrounding bush.

PAGE 78: The dining room bar trolley with brass casters is composed of a dark stained rattan from Pacific Traders Cebu. The wooden mirror above it reflects the panoramic views outside.

PAGE 79: We truly enjoy our sundowners, or happy hour in South Africa's bush, whether indoors or out. Here, I set up Melvill & Moon walnut Roorkhee chairs in olive canvas and a kilim for those who want to lounge on the grass.

LEFT: For the house's roof, we decided on a simple covering of corrugated steel in a rust color to blend with the oxidized soil of the surrounding landscape. We also maintain a large lawn in which the kids can play safely. This garden was one of the best decisions we made—a wonderful and much-loved addition to our home where we play catch, croquet, football, cricket, tag, slip and slide, and other fun games.

FOLLOWING SPREAD: The dining room is cozy with its clad stone walls and lath ceiling. While the room feels naturalistic in its design, the brass shelving and crystal chandelier add a touch of elegance to the space. The solid oval oak table was custom made by Philux and the chairs are a Filipino rattan rendition of the classic director's chair. Distressed chocolate leather cushions and bar stools make for comfortable sitting after long game drives.

THIS PAGE: Lapalala Wilderness is home to the Big Five (lion, leopard, rhinoceros, buffalo, and elephant), which have been illustrated in the works of early San bushmen found in secluded cliff overhangs and caves along the meandering Palala River. I have seen four of them there—the elusive leopard still escapes me. I am inspired by the colors and textures of the animals, including the zebra, European bee-eater, and lion.

ABOVE: On the wall of the breezeway are photographs taken by Chris of some of these magnificent animals.

FOLLOWING SPREAD: Sunlight floods the main bedroom throughout the day. There is no shortage of natural elements in this room—a four-poster bed made in the Philippines with a headboard wrapped in jute rope, cabinets lined with seagrass wallpaper, a rustic reed ceiling, and woven and vintage Berber rugs. A subtle palette of hues, including soft almond, bone, dove gray, and touches of black, provides a sense of calm to our private sanctuary.

RIGHT: The outdoor terrace, or lanai as we say in the Philippines, with its natural textures and earthy color palette, offers a peaceful spot that blends seamlessly with the outdoors.

PAGE 90: Behind the bed in the main bedroom is a cozy yet functional area. An oversize oak dresser accessorized with African objects and a vase of fresh proteas allows for ample storage space. Across from it, a washed leopard-print upholstered bench is used for putting on safari boots.

PAGE 91: A bathtub with a view was my nonnegotiable for the house. Sliding doors in the main bathroom allow for a liberating outdoor feeling. My afternoon baths are sacred and many a time I catch sight of a herd of kudu approaching the water hole. The scene is romantic— and almost comically surreal.

LEFT: While Modumela remains faithful to the natural surroundings, I did add vibrance to the girls' room by painting it in peach, with elements in green, and mustard tones. The Ardmore Singita accent wallpaper between the built-in cabinets adds playfulness, while the colorful African baskets bring another texture to the room. The Philux whitewashed wooden beds are a modern take on a Victorian metal bed design; their trundles are a functional feature for sleepovers.

PAGE 94: The covered terrace adjacent to the den welcomes long views of the plains. It is decorated with woven furniture with pops of color. The small pillow fabric was salvaged from a kilim. The coffee table is a vintage African daybed.

93

PAGE 95 AND OPPOSITE: The roof garden pathway is lined with overgrown grass and succulents. It is located above the kitchen and functions as a transitional space that boasts beautiful views while linking the den of the main house to the private guest suites nestled in the hill. My girls enjoy exploring the property—it is a large, wild playground for them.

PREVIOUS SPREAD: The family den is a cozy space that hosts a television, books, games, and comfortable seating—it is a nice retreat for the kids when the outdoors is blazing hot.

ABOVE: I sometimes move a table outside for alfresco entertaining. Drinks and nibbles cap a beautiful day.

LEFT: Our powder room features an Elitis wallpaper, a natural wood edged counter, a brass sink, and bronze fixtures by Victorian Bathrooms. A few of my favorite Africology skincare products (they are natural, eco-friendly, and scented with essential oils) complete this private space.

OPPOSITE: Our home's staircase has become an homage to the wonderful moments and people in our lives. Photographs of my late Grany, Lolo Daning, Chris's mom, Terry, and his grandfather Lolo Pocholo keep their spirits alive.

PAGES 102–107: The guest suites were designed with complete privacy in mind. We want our guests to feel attuned to the natural surroundings to be able to fully unwind. While still cozy in size, each guest room has expansive views of the bush, a wraparound terrace, and outdoor shower. The oak four-poster beds were designed and manufactured by Philux. It is important to me to include a piece of the Philippines, my heritage, in every space of the home.

ENTERTAINING

Indoor Entertaining

Few things in life are as satisfying as sharing a meal and an intimate conversation with another. This is what I find beautiful about entertaining: the opportunity to connect with someone in a private and personal setting. It is a sensory experience, with all elements—from the food and the drinks, to the lighting, the music, and the scent—playing a role in setting the mood for the occasion.

When entertaining indoors, I always start with an apéritif and some light canapés around our foyer table, and I play soft jazz or bossa nova. I light my favorite candles. These elements conjure specific and cherished memories—for instance, the rich smell of Mom's coq au vin simmering in the kitchen.

I like to add an element of surprise when entertaining—something as simple as moving the dining area to a different location. My favorite nights include those where we transform our coffee table into an evening picnic spot. We use a plaid tablecloth and change up the serving ware and cutlery, setting the scene for a boisterous dinner with our children before we settle down for family movie night.

PAGE 108: Marie Daâge hand-painted plates are paired with a petrified wood charger and ombre linen napkins. A beetle in stone and brass functions as a napkin ring and green hydrangeas add a calming accent to the table.

PAGE 109: A beautiful sunset in Lapalala is always enjoyed more with drinks and appetizers, surrounded by good company.

OPPOSITE: Table scapes are a great way to channel your creativity. The art of gathering community around a table has always been a passion of mine. Here, chartreuse linen napkins are held by Philux's mother-of-pearl rings. Gold-plated bamboo cutlery by Alain Saint Joanis flanks beaded zebra print chargers by Kim Seybert and ocher plates by Aarde.

RIGHT: I am always looking for ways to create warmth and beauty at home. Nature is my main source of inspiration— floral arrangements enliven an entertaining setting. There are many moods you can express with blooms, and while I love a sumptuous table, my favorite compositions exercise restraint and highlight elegant simplicity.

FOLLOWING SPREAD: A Filipino *merienda*, or afternoon snack is always a tropical feast for the senses where tabletop accessories, flowers, and food are unified. Bright orchids, bromeliads, seasonal fruit, leaves, driftwood, and local textiles can all play a role at the table. I usually serve local crowd favorites such as *bibingka* (salted egg rice cakes) and *pancit luglug* (a saucy dish served with seafood garnish, spring onions, and thick rice noodles).

ABOVE: Sundowner drinks form part of the ultimate bush safari experience. I had a custom rattan bar trolley designed in the Philippines to house our spirits and mixology books.

OPPOSITE: Bright and spacious, our Modumela kitchen is anchored by a large white island where anyone can assist with food preparation. I opted for white subway tiles and a terrazzo floor for ease of maintenance.

LEFT: For formal occasions, you cannot go wrong with a traditional setting composed of a crisp white tablecloth, crystal, and silver cutlery. This table is adorned with a singular central arrangement of white amaryllis, greens, and tall gold candles. While the design of the table is classic, certain elements such as the rolled napkin presentation and the handcrafted plates add a touch of modernity.

OPPOSITE: I love mixing modern and traditional elements—here, monochromatic Carrara plates from Vista Alegre, Portugal in a contemporary design are paired with vintage silver, including my mother-in-law's cutlery, which gives a lovely sense of history.

ABOVE: I lean towards a more feminine palette for a lunch with the ladies: pastels, floral napkins, a touch of green in the Alain Saint Joanis cutlery and local rattan woven chargers to bring an artisanal element to the elegant table scape.

Outdoor Entertaining

While I adore a beautiful meal indoors, there is nothing I enjoy more than outdoor dining on a picturesque day. I set a table with linen napkins, handcrafted ceramic plates, my go-to Laguiole cutlery, woven place mats, and serve colorful, nourishing dishes adorned with blooms and greens in various vessels. *L'art de la table* is my playtime, and I relish the sounds of my children splashing around the pool on a sunny, breezy morning as I create a beautiful table scape.

The natural elements—from the weather to the surrounding wildlife—play such an important role in the whole experience of dining outside. You can never control the breeze, the heat, or the chirping birds, and while this sometimes does not work in your favor, when it does, it proves simply magical.

For lunches, I always serve a cooling refreshment in the summer—our homemade strawberry iced tea is a crowd-pleaser. A rainbow of colors adorns the table—starting with the bread served in a woven bowl and the butter in a traditional silver container. I often place casual and more classic elements side by side. I serve salads composed of rich greens, reds, oranges, fruit, grains, and cheese along with some form of protein and starch—whether seafood or meat and pasta or a whole-grain rice salad. Fruit kebabs make for the perfect end to a summery meal under the pergola.

OPPOSITE: Our sunken deck, located in a corner of the property, is a spot where we linger mid-morning with a cup of coffee in hand, midday to catch some sun, and in the evening around a fire. The large pillows are covered in traditional African fabrics and the seating and matching back cushions are upholstered in outdoor waterproof material that is easy to maintain. A large aloe adds a sculptural element to the setting.

LEFT AND OPPOSITE: Eating outdoors is synonymous with holidays for me. There is nothing like a shared meal alfresco on a glorious, sunny day. The shaded poolside porch at the end of our lawn is the preferred spot. Very often, the kids jump straight into the pool while the adults finish off with a refreshing fruit-based dessert and coffee. We planted wild jasmine vines around the porch's support poles, and I look forward to when they cover the entire roof with their fragrant leaves.

PAGE 126: A classic blue-and-white table setting: The blue-and-white protea plates are from Mervyn Gers and the cutlery is Laguiole. Silver pieces are a lovely complement to this setup. Refreshing colorful salads and iced drinks are served outside.

PAGE 127: On a sunny day, there is nothing more delightful than dining together in the garden under the shade of the pergola.

RIGHT: On cooler days, we prepare a sumptuous brunch on the covered terrace. On the chair backs are green throws from Mungo—cozy on cool days.

PAGE 130: This afternoon tea setup is adorned with African patterns in tones of blue—a modern twist to the classic blue-and-white theme. The tea set is vintage silver with rattan accents.

PAGE 131: Woven chairs and a metal-base table are perfect for this casual outdoor spot. I use custom covers to protect my outdoor furnishings when they are not in use to ensure their longevity.

PREVIOUS SPREAD: Sundowners by the lawn and deck are always a joy to set up. A kilim is laid flat on the grass with pillows scattered over it. An antique daybed and vintage spotted rattan tables are brought out for casual seating and to hold food and drinks. The walnut field bar by Melvill & Moon is open for business, and canapés are served on rustic wood platters as we enjoy the African sunset.

ABOVE AND OPPOSITE: I like to add color to my tables when entertaining. The varied shades of the blooms and the fresh food make mealtimes more vibrant. The elements of the table complement the natural surroundings.

PAGES 136 AND 137: Our *boma* (traditionally known as an enclosure to protect livestock from the elements) is a magical setting for gathering around the fire under the stars. We delight in these evenings outdoors where we *braai* (Afrikaans for barbecue or roast) and serve hearty oxtail stew in *potjies*, or three-legged pots. My girls always request toasted marshmallows to cap the meals.

LEFT: This walnut field bar is from Melvill & Moon. It can be transported to any area of the house to create an instant traditional safari ambience.

OPPOSITE: For romantic evening outdoor dining, our round table is moved to the middle of the lawn and covered with a Hessian textured tablecloth. A firepit prepared nearby sets the tone.

INSPIRING CREATIVES

DESIGNERS AND TASTEMAKERS
WHO HAVE MOVED ME

Over the years I've turned to the expertise and knowledge of many of the best designers and tastemakers working today for a fresh take on decorating, entertaining, gardening, and art. As my ethos is conscious living, I am naturally drawn to creatives who share my outlook. Several have imparted invaluable advice to me regarding the process of designing a home, from the fundamentals to the finishing touches. Others have collaborated with me on personal projects such as the construction of my environmentally conscious retreat surrounded by sustainable landscaping.

Here are brief profiles of a few of my creative collaborators as well as their advice for achieving great design. I look to this group—who hail from points as diverse as America, South Africa, and the Philippines—for their practical tips, artistry, and thought-provoking design to bring natural elements into the home.

PAGE 140: A serene moment at Londolozi private game reserve in Sabi Sands, South Africa, where the interiors blend seamlessly with the wild surroundings.

PAGE 141: A vignette of rough and honed textures and greenery adds interest to any tabletop.

RIGHT: Yvonne O'Brien's seating area at South Africa's Londolozi Granite Camp was inspired by the color and rugged texture of elephant hides. The Zulu word *londolozi* means "protector of all living things."

Yvonne O'Brien

Chris and I were drawn to the work of Yvonne O'Brien of the Private House Company because of her knack for mixing natural materials with a contemporary vision. Her flair for juxtaposing the old and the new dovetails with my own design philosophy, making her the ideal choice as a co-designer for Modumela House. I had complete confidence in O'Brien's abilities to interpret my vision: I wanted to integrate my love of Africa with my affection for the Philippines, and the best way to do so was by creating a layered look that incorporated Filipino decor.

O'Brien graduated from the KLC School of Design in London, returning home to South Africa to sell items she had collected on her travels. Over twenty years ago, she opened the Private House, which is now based in Sandton, Johannesburg's design district. Although the company still offers a carefully curated and personally sourced range of furniture and home decor, it also provides a turnkey design service.

Since she has worked extensively at game lodges, it's not surprising that the African landscape helped shape O'Brien's aesthetic. Nature and the play of light across the continent's plains have been especially influential since she favors interiors bathed in natural light. She also delights in incorporating both the patterns and the materials of this special land: rattan, baskets, and sisal, for example, or zebra skin and bronze anklets. Drawn to contrast, she juxtaposes opposing elements, offsetting something antique and aged with a fresh and novel item.

Chris and I are both great believers in the power of sentiment as a design element. O'Brien creates sanctuaries for her clients, filled with much-loved objects that nurture the soul and reflect what is beautiful, rather than what is on trend. Her spaces are easy to live in—and, although each room possesses its own character, the spaces are united by a common thread. She believes in giving a room time to take shape in her mind, but once she finds her inspiration, it generally grows, unfettered, taking on a life of its own.

One of the ways O'Brien achieves calm is by keeping interiors clean, with a restrained use of color. That's not to say her spaces are bland— far from it: she enjoys creating interest by layering diverse textures and objects. This enhances the room's personality without disturbing that all-important serenity.

O'Brien tries to foster a connection with nature through her designs. It is an ethos she believes is certain to take root since many people seem far less attached to their belongings than they once were. Ultimately, O'Brien believes that the purpose of design is to unite form, function, and sentiment in a space both thoughtful and meaningful.

OPPOSITE: The home study in a house in Steyn City, Johannesburg, is a blend of contemporary pieces and objects from the South African bush. Clean lines and a neutral palette are mixed with luxurious finishes and organic textures.

OPPOSITE AND ABOVE: At the Londolozi Founders Camp, the spaces feature a layering of neutral colors and are laid back and playful, while the game reserve's Tree Camp is more formal. Inspired by the renowned Londolozi leopards, the color scheme is a mix of white, chocolate, and a pale brown, like an aged leadwood tree.

Tim Steyn

We were excited to welcome Tim Steyn, born into a family of renowned gardeners, into the Modumela House team. His belief that every garden has a soul is fundamental to his approach, guiding him to blend bush and structured landscape into a seamless whole on our property.

Steyn has a rare talent for transforming raw sites into verdant, living gardens—a skill he learned from his mother, Elizabeth Steyn, whose high-profile career spanned thirty years. It was Elizabeth who nurtured Tim's belief that a space comes alive with the introduction of greenery. He believes that, with more of the planet given over to urbanization, this is becoming especially important.

Steyn points to the growing awareness of the benefits of spending time outdoors, which has encouraged architects to integrate landscapes into their designs. Technological advances have also helped; even if you don't have space for large flower beds and sprawling lawns, you can still enhance your space with a green roof, green wall, or indoor planting.

And if it is maintenance, rather than space, that poses a hurdle, pots and containers are the answer. Steyn notes that they make it possible to introduce verdant touches throughout the house without much effort. The key is to start with the basics: good soil, adequate light, and expert advice. Wood or steel planters suit a range of aesthetics, and from here it is possible to build on plantings.

Steyn draws inspiration from the play of light, form, texture, and rhythm. His goal, always, is to design a space that radiates peace and tranquility, especially during the hours that enjoy soft light. He strives to create harmony between a building and its surroundings so that each client feels a connection to the site, and every garden has a gravity point through the use of specific planting styles, or by introducing elements like water into the arrangement.

But it is not just about aesthetics. Sustainability and practicality are very much part of Steyn's design ethos. He likens his process to that of a sculptor hewing stone; as he works, he discards unnecessary elements and strives for simplicity wherever possible. His ideas come from myriad sources: the way sunlight bounces off the bark off a tree, for example, or how a rock looks when wet. He makes a point of visiting his sites at all hours to see what they look like as the light changes—conscious, always, that his work is ephemeral and what has been easily created may be destroyed by something as seemingly inconsequential as a hailstorm.

Steyn's work is satisfying in so many ways: there's the joy that comes from transforming a raw, formless site into a place of beauty that gives people pleasure. There's also the integral connection with the seasonality of life, and the cycles and rhythms we humans experience. Above all, there is the beauty found in the smallest things—if only we take time to look.

OPPOSITE: A conversation pit around a fire in a garden in Sandhurst, Johannesburg. The purple colors from the jacaranda tree blossoms bleed down into the lavender and statice plantings below. This is a lovely, relaxed area for happy hour drinks on a summer evening.

FOLLOWING SPREAD: A beautiful pool high up on Westcliff Ridge in Johannesburg, overlooking the city. Veld grasses create a natural and indigenous feel to the garden.

Lionel Smit

I discovered the work of South African artist Lionel Smit while honeymooning with Chris in Cape Town. We were touring the Delaire Graff Estate when we came upon a large, evocative artwork. We were struck by the modernity of the art around us, juxtaposed against the background of the looming Stellenbosch mountains. Smit's piercing portrait, hanging above the winery's reception, made a particular impression, thanks to his use of bold abstract strokes in rich colors and subtle, yet emotive, facial expressions. We instantly became fans.

We have since visited Smit's studio, marveling at his moving paintings and bronze sculptures. We were thrilled to purchase a large portrait, which hangs in our double-height living room in Manila. It is a special piece that we love for its unexpected proportions, soothing color palette, and striking appearance.

Smit's oversize portraits and sculptures—all inspired by the human form—have been exhibited in South Africa, London, Miami, Vermont, and New York. In 2013, he won the Visitors' Choice Award at the BP Portrait Award competition at London's National Portrait Gallery and the Ministerial Award from the Department of Culture for Visual Art. His favorite project is *Obscura*, hosted by the Museum of Contemporary Art North Miami, which explores the concept of multiethnicity and how we are shaped—and placed—by our identity. This was the first time Smit developed an extensive solo exhibition with a specific space in mind, and he relished the challenge of creating a multidisciplinary exhibition with different mediums—including painting, sculpture, paper, installation, and video—all communicating.

Smit spent much of his Pretoria childhood in his father's studio. But, while Anton Smit was a self-taught sculptor, Lionel went on to attend the Pro Arte School of the Arts. His style, subject, and inspiration are constantly evolving. Smit doesn't attempt to evoke any particular message through his art—a mission he believes would be foolhardy given that art is subjective, with viewers' perceptions shaped by their interpretation, emotion, and experience of a piece. This, in turn, is influenced by a viewer's identity—a subject that is a strong recurring theme in Smit's own work, thanks to his fascination with emotion and how the human experience connects us all.

OPPOSITE: Lionel Smit's painting *Divide* hangs in Delaire Graff Estate's stunning tasting room in the Stellenbosch Winelands of South Africa. The top half is more complete in the traditional sense, while the bottom half exposes the rawness of the painting process.

RIGHT: A view of Smit's studio showcasing works ready for his exhibition, *Discrepancies*, at the Uitstalling Art Gallery, Belgium. This part of his studio space is dedicated to works in progress.

Fernando Zóbel de Ayala

BUSINESSMAN, ART COLLECTOR, AND PATRON OF THE ARTS, MANILA, THE PHILIPPINES

While he is best known as a leading figure in Philippine business, Fernando Zóbel de Ayala is also an ardent advocate of culture and the arts. I have a great respect for his work in elevating the arts scene in my home country. He started collecting art as a teenager, searching through Europe's weekend markets for hidden gems on a meager budget. This passion for the arts was nurtured at an early age and bolstered by a supportive family. Trips included visits to museums. His aunt, Mercedes Zóbel, and her husband, Joseph McMicking, prepared the groundwork for what was to become the Ayala Museum and the Ayala Foundation Inc., institutions that carry the mission of instilling pride in Filipino culture, traditions, and history.

Presently, he chairs the Ayala Museum, an institution dedicated to the preservation, interpretation, and study of Filipino art and culture through its collections of precolonial gold, Asian ceramics, indigenous textiles, and fine arts. He supports Art Fair Philippines, a platform for the best of Philippine contemporary art. He takes this fervor for the arts internationally in his engagements on committees with the Tate Modern in London and the Metropolitan Museum of Art in New York.

He is the namesake and godson of Fernando Zóbel de Ayala y Montojo, a painter active in the arts scene in Manila and Spain from the 1950s to the early 1980s. I have long admired the painter Fernando, who was one of the pioneering abstractionists in Philippine modern art. His artistic output, from semiabstract to pure nonobjective, shows both dynamism and tranquility. We are fortunate to have one of his abstract oils hanging in our dining room.

Today, the younger Fernando's personal art collection has greatly evolved, with the works of his great-uncle remaining key elements. He has two favorite pieces: *Saeta Granadina* (1959), a transitional work featuring aspects of both the artist's earlier *Saeta* period and from the iconic *Serie Negra* paintings; and the Murillo-Velarde Map, which dates to 1734 and is the first scientific map of the Philippine archipelago during the Spanish colonial period. The historic map not only documents the country's territory through the work of cartographer Pedro Murillo-Velarde, a Jesuit priest, but it also showcases the work of local engraver and printer Nicholas de la Cruz Bagay, as well as the inhabitants, flora, and fauna of the archipelago in the images rendered by another local engraver named Francisco Suarez.

For Fernando Zóbel de Ayala, supporting the arts and starting a collection is a personal exercise. He advises new and existing collectors to know what moves and excites them, and to explore various art forms, artistic movements, and local and international artists. He also believes that visual sensibility and an understanding of the world's civilizations invigorate and inform the pursuit of objects of beauty, history, and meaning.

OPPOSITE: Fernando Zóbel de Ayala's favorite painting from his collection is the 1959 *Saeta Granadina* (over the couch) by his grand-uncle Fernando Zóbel de Ayala Montojo.

157

Olivia d'Aboville

I have always looked up to French-Filipino artist and designer Olivia d'Aboville—whom I am fortunate to call a dear friend—for her authenticity: she has stayed true to her mission of creating art that speaks of nature, hope, conservation, beauty, and humanity. D'Aboville's art is an amalgamation of all these concepts. She explores the relationship between the organic and the synthetic through her mode of expression, working predominantly with Philippine fibers or recycled and upcycled materials that reflect her concerns for the environment. The resulting pieces, which have been exhibited in Manila, Paris, Lyon, Hong Kong, Shanghai, Singapore, and New York, are as delicate and fragile as the environment itself—and a tangible expression of d'Aboville's role as its advocate.

D'Aboville has come to be known especially for her work with handwoven abaca, which she pleats into textile artworks. She was introduced to her signature material by her weaving mentor, Francis Dravigny of Cebu Interlace, in 2015. The handwoven, hand-dyed silk shibori made by the Rurungan Sa Tubod Foundation of Palawan is another favorite material. The appeal of these fabrics lies in their story: each piece represents an enormous investment in both time and labor and, because of this, each feels special.

Sustainability has always been at the core of d'Aboville's work and lifestyle, giving credence to her belief that creativity and eco-consciousness can coexist. It all begins with an awareness of the materials used, their provenance, and how much of the earth's resources have been exploited to make them. This ethos guides her own work: she makes a point of investigating the origins of all materials she works with, who made them, what will happen to them years from now, and whether any communities have been impacted during production. She experiments with new materials, from glass to Stonecast (crushed limestone) and Nucast (compressed paper pulp)—products created by Nature's Legacy in Cebu. These materials are ideal for permanent outdoor displays, allowing her to create sculptural works that are durable and large in scale. D'Aboville has also experimented with digital printing on abaca polyester textiles with sublimation dye.

She is certain that sustainable art—or, rather, making art with sustainable materials—is here to stay; sustainability is, after all, a cornerstone of the future well-being of communities and the environment alike. At the same time, she is charmed by the ephemeral nature of art, believing that there is something poetic about the slow degradation of her works.

OPPOSITE: Olivia d'Aboville working on *Flower of Life*, a piece commissioned by the Peninsula Manila's Pink event, a campaign for breast cancer awareness.

LEFT: Her famous sculptural piece, *Giant Dandelions*, in full bloom in the evening at the GLOW light art festival, Eindhoven, The Netherlands. This lighting installation, composed of a forest of ninety larger-than-life dandelions made of approximately 9,000 recycled plastic bottles, has color-changing LED strips.

Bea and Marga Valdes

I have known Bea and Marga Valdes for many years and have been greatly inspired by their craft. From fashion to art and soft interior furnishings, they approach each project with purpose. Since the company's launch, Bea Valdes's work has been featured in international magazines, and the sisters have collaborated with a number of leading brands, including Roche Bobois and Swarovski. For me, it has been a pleasure working with them on a Philux home furnishings collection that is accented with their signature hand-beading, hand-painting, and embroidery.

The Valdes sisters have a singular point of view, often saying that "nothing connects us with humanity quite so gently as working with our hands." This insight developed naturally around their grandmother's table, which was frequently adorned by a special mantle—a traditional tablecloth made from the delicate pineapple fiber, piña, for which the Philippines is known. The mantle featured beautiful, hand-embroidered motifs, and even as children, the Valdes sisters noticed its fragile beauty. They were moved too by the community of women who would spend many months working side by side to complete such pieces. The idea of women coming together, creating in unison, has had an enormous impact on the sisters, sparking a lifelong fascination with the heritage of local craft.

Their unique definition of Filipino craft translates across a range of mediums—from furniture to fashion. They never stray from their approach, which hinges on slow design emphasizing the artisan's handwork. They believe that every crafter needs to continuously hone their craft, seeking different perspectives that may inform their journey while remaining authentic in their artistic intention. The way they manipulate materials reflects their personal stories. And, in turn, the sisters create timeless heirlooms that will be passed from one generation to another. These pieces also maintain relevance in an ever-changing world.

OPPOSITE: Bea and Marga Valdes's *Evening Lily* hangs in the Shangri-La Hotel in Colombo, Sri Lanka. This fabric artwork is composed of individually hand-sewn satin petals, each independently assembled.

ABOVE: The bespoke Luna chair is a Philux Bea Valdes collaboration for Louis Vuitton's flagship store in Manilla. Inspired by the natural fibers and textures from the Philippine Islands, the luxurious sustainable embroideries were developed using zero waste appliqués that embody conscious crafting.

OPPOSITE: From the Philux Hearth Collection, these vibrant Bea Valdes chairs have hand-painted linen seat cushions with chain and sequin appliqués.

Kenneth Cobonpue

I have always looked up to industrial designer Kenneth Cobonpue. His playful design savvy is appreciated in all corners of the world, and many Filipinos—including myself—take pride in his success. With his creative interpretations of nature, Cobonpue transports us to a place of fantasy and imagination.

Cobonpue's concept of design as something that inspires happiness was shaped during his childhood: playing in his mother's furniture workshop, he would collect scraps of wood, rattan, and fabric, using them to fashion his own toys, and basking in the smiles his objects elicited from his mother. Cobonpue realized that he'd found his element with design.

While Cobonpue's craft has evolved, his design ethos remains constant—it should provide fresh and unique solutions to everyday problems. What has not changed is Cobonpue's deep respect for natural materials. He loves that a chair might remind someone of a beautiful seascape, a wonderful holiday, or summer in the forest.

He is equally inspired by craftsmanship, the driving force behind his designs and one of his company's key differentiators. Since craftsmanship is such an integral part of Filipino culture, we must preserve it and make sure that new generations can earn a living from carving, weaving, and building things by hand. Cobonpue hopes to see the country's aesthetic become global.

His advice to other crafters? Keep an open mind. Cobonpue says that he always looks for the good in what others present, whether he is speaking to a junior designer new to the job or to a craftsperson to whom he is demonstrating a technique. The craftsperson may uncover a better way to accomplish things, or even just provide a new spark of inspiration—but, either way, Cobonpue is richer for the experience.

OPPOSITE: Kenneth Cobonpue's Voyage Bed is dreamy and reminiscent of papyrus and reed boats.

Elora Hardy

Seeing Elora Hardy's passion for bamboo come to life at the Green Village in Ubud, Bali, was a wonderful privilege. This harmonious resort community—twelve homes in a valley along the Ayung River—was built entirely from the humble material, and it is remarkable to see it transformed into beautiful, modern architecture. I was entirely awestruck by Hardy's design and inspired to see how bamboo can be honed so beautifully and sustainably, rooting itself to the earth in a variety of ways.

Founder and creative director of the green design firm IBUKU, Hardy has helped establish Bali's reputation as a center of sustainable design. Her work, inspired by the craftspeople and culture of Bali, has been recognized by *Architectural Digest*, which named her an AD Innovator in 2013, as well as the Royal Society of Arts, which awarded her the Honorary Royal Designer for Industry in 2019.

Hardy returned to Bali in 2010 after moving to the United States at the age of fourteen to go to boarding school. She then received a degree in fine arts and worked in the fashion industry where she most notably designed prints for Donna Karan. In 2010, Hardy returned to Bali to help her jewelry designer father, John Hardy, and his wife, Cynthia Hardy, design Green Village, a community of bamboo homes. She was drawn to bamboo for its strength and flexibility. More than this, it is the world's most environmentally friendly building material, with a four-year growth cycle. Hardy looks to bamboo as something that can be counted on, even into the future; it grows quickly for years. The material guides her design process, firing her imagination and helping her find the wisdom to seek its possibilities. In this way, bamboo connects her to nature.

Hardy's residential architectural designs consider how she can provide just the right amount of shelter. For example, at the Green Village, spaces like the master bedroom incorporate private enclosures, but communal areas are characterized by open space so that inhabitants can experience Hardy's favorite luxuries: the breeze, the sound of the wind through the leaves, birdsongs, or the way the light falls across the floor.

Making decisions and choosing materials in line with maintaining a healthy and beautiful world are at the core of everything she does. Her work is not meant to be appreciated aesthetically, she says—it is more about how it makes people feel and how it changes them.

OPPOSITE: At a secluded edge of Bambu Indah's valley, Elora Hardy's design firm, IBUKU, was commissioned in 2019 to design Riverbend House, a cozy two-bedroom home in the natural setting of rice terraces and lotus ponds. The construction of the nest or basketlike spaces using beams to cross each other feels in keeping with the river setting.

ABOVE: Moon House at Bambu Indah, an eco-resort in Sayan, Bali, was codesigned by Elora Hardy and her father, John Hardy, in 2017 to give guests a connection to "the pulse of nature" while maintaining luxurious features. Enveloped by a curving roof, but open to the elements, the bed can also be enclosed and air-conditioned to provide the best of both worlds. Its orientation conforms to the Balinese tradition of aligning the sleeping person's head toward sacred Mount Agung.

RIGHT: The handcrafted bamboo chair, designed by IBUKU and made by Bamboo Pure craftsmen, takes in the view of the grotto pool.

OPPOSITE: Cacao House at Green Village, Bali, is an elegant three-story, three-bedroom bamboo house built within a wild cacao grove. The kitchen and furniture are made of bamboo.

ABOVE: Conceived by John Hardy in 2009, Green Village is a community of private homes neighboring the Green School in Bali. The master plan was developed by the PT Bamboo Pure team—Putra Wiarsa, Nyoman Kerta, Macarena Chiriboga, and Effan Adhiwira. Designed by the team that founded IBUKU, Palm House at Green Village, a five-story, three-bedroom house, was built in 2010 on the edge of the river valley among the coconut trees.

OPPOSITE: Instead of a railing, the Moon House at Bambu Indah has a hammock net that wraps around it, above the spring-fed freshwater plunge pool designed with river stones to appear like a grotto.

Hadley Wiggins-Marin

INTERIOR DESIGNER AND ANTIQUES COLLECTOR, NEW YORK CITY, NEW YORK, USA

OPPOSITE: The screened-in porch of this home on the East End of Long Island is filled with vintage furnishings, including a rattan sofa and kilim. The painted green floor is a bit more special than the expected gray. Hadley Wiggins-Marin chose a tonal fabric for the sofa and chair cushions to provide a sense of calm.

PAGE 176: For the renovation of this Brooklyn brownstone, Wiggins-Marin brought back its history by sourcing period mantels in England and replicating picture moldings and plaster crown moldings. The rooms' subtle tones are punctuated by rich fabrics and woods. Washed-out Turkish rugs float on the white oak floors.

PAGE 177: The walls of a guest cottage kitchen on the East End of Long Island are covered in William Morris Willow Bough wallpaper, juxtaposed against a mid-century table and chairs. The common thread is found through the harmony of shape and mood.

I met Hadley Wiggins-Marin when we were both studying at Sarah Lawrence College in New York. We bonded over our interests in wellness and beautiful homes, and both decided to study art history. I'm not surprised that we have found our niche in the same industry. Even though we live and work on opposite sides of the world—me making furniture in the Philippines, while she is a collector and designer living in New York—we remain connected through our undiminished passion for creating beautiful, warm, meaningful spaces.

Wiggins-Marin describes herself as a self-taught interior designer. She grew up with a deep appreciation for living in an environment imbued with meaning, and for the positive impact a well-designed home has on one's well-being. Her design business, Hadley Wiggins Inc., established in 2012, operates alongside an antiques store, which makes it possible for her to sell pieces collected during her travels or use them in client projects.

Wiggins-Marin is drawn to antiques because she believes they are like sculptures. Old items carry their own history—an energy from the people and places who loved and appreciated them in the past. A piece may be measured and found valuable for different reasons: for its aesthetic appeal, its rareness, or the material from which it is made. Blending these pieces with other items, collected over a lifetime and sourced from every corner of the globe, makes for spaces filled with history, stories, and diversity. The items Wiggins-Marin uses, disparate though they may be, are always linked by a harmonious thread. The result: interiors that reflect a belief that history and use—and reuse—are an integral part of beauty, and that authenticity is intrinsic to value.

For Wiggins-Marin, homes should reflect what their owners find inspiring and where they see beauty. Decor and furnishings should create a mood and can evoke the feelings and memories of places and times past, or even from the imagination.

Perfection has no place in Wiggins-Marin's designs. Her definition of a beautiful home is one that's livable, one that has room for kids and dogs and muddy boots. It should be adaptable for future additions or changes, for the items that enter life and become part of the tapestry of memory. This is why Wiggins-Marin doesn't believe in rigid matching and coordination. Instead, she treats spaces as evolving, reflecting changing lifestyles. As part of this, she allows for moments of aspiration, always looking ahead to the future of a space—the inclusion of a precious white sofa, a cherished rug, a coaster-only table, pieces that add to the elusive balance of lived-in beauty.

India Hicks

OPPOSITE: Layering natural accents in a garage setting in England—wooden hurricanes, woven grass chargers, and foldable chairs—adds a feeling of coziness. The last of the summer slipped away as the candles were lit during this memorable evening.

PAGE 180: Classic blue and white does not have to be precious— here, in an elegant setting, the table is set with mismatched plates from an antiques shop in England. The bamboo candlesticks add a tropical element to the mix.

PAGE 181: "A romantic setting can be conjured anywhere," says India Hicks. At the end of a dock, a table covered in a charming printed tablecloth and topped with a chandelier and a pitcher of roses has been set up for enjoying a bottle of chilled champagne.

I have always admired India Hicks for her chic, laid-back style. Her love affair with the Bahamas reminds me of my own fascination with South Africa. Rooted in family, and a philanthropic sense of purpose, Hicks's endeavors, no matter how big or small, always delight. Her effortless take on entertaining is full of creativity.

Her flair as a hostess is inherited; her grandparents were always entertaining, as were her parents. Brought up in this atmosphere of warmth and hospitality, she developed her own innate style—never roaming far from the feeling that no matter what the occasion, whether a simple supper, a lively lunch, or a fundraising dinner, every gathering should have the intimacy and joy of a family affair.

She's particularly talented when it comes to creating an ambience. For this, she relies on magnificent table settings, enjoying the challenge of thinking up new decorations or even moving locations—from barns to beaches—to inject novelty and excitement into her get-togethers. Her tables always pay tribute to their location, usually in the form of decor borrowed from the surroundings. For instance, at her home in the Bahamas, guests may find their place setting sprinkled with "lucky" nuts collected from the beach, while palm fronds trail from tall vases. In England, small posies of English roses or pots of lavender or wild thistles bring a touch of the fields to the table. Even duvet covers and scarves have been pulled into service as tablecloths.

Hicks makes a point of involving as many of her children as possible in setting the table. She often asks them to help decorate cakes. Although the result is far less polished than it would be if a professional had assisted, that is the very point: She loves the slightly haphazard outcomes of her family's efforts, believing that this enhances the intimacy of the event. But while she sticks to the tried and trusted for menu options, themes and settings are ever changing. While it may sound daunting to come up with new inspiration for every gathering, Hicks says that quite the opposite is true: once you have dreamed up a theme, you'll find elements that would fit in everywhere you look. She cites rose gold as an example. For daughter Domino's eighth birthday celebration, she found everything from a rose-gold microphone for karaoke to rose-gold flared candles.

Although Hicks has some key tips for success—an ice-breaking drink is a must, and you can never have too many tea lights—she's also relaxed enough to let the occasion take its course, understanding that even the most well-planned event could be sabotaged by the unexpected. This is something she has learned from personal experience: once, having invited the king of Spain to dinner, she was confused when he didn't arrive— only to realize that they had both muddled the date.

Nate Berkus and Lauren Buxbaum Gordon

I have followed the work of interior designer team Nate Berkus and Lauren Buxbaum Gordon of Nate Berkus Associates for some time. Their impeccable layering of contemporary and classic creates the perfect counterpoint, bringing wonderful energy and warmth to a room. While they usually gravitate toward neutral palettes, their projects are brought to life with incredible textures, patina, conversation pieces, and rich, natural materials. They use sustainable materials like wicker, seagrass, and raffia, and add greenery including branches, potted trees, and fresh flowers.

A love of design was woven into both Berkus's and Buxbaum Gordon's childhoods. In Berkus's case, he inherited the passion from his interior designer mother, who filled the house with wallpaper books and fabric samples. Buxbaum Gordon's experience wasn't very different: she, too, inherited an eye from her parents, who were art dealers. Like me, Berkus says that he places high value on attributes such as character and age; vintage lighting, architectural salvage, and other components allow him to tell a story through design. Provenance is all important in his eyes; every piece sourced is interrogated so that he knows who made it, how it was made, and if it was inspired by something handcrafted.

Buxbaum Gordon strives to create tension between traditional and modern in each space but doesn't overthink things. Rather, her design process is creative and organic, instinctual rather than formulaic. One of the ways she achieves this effortless blend of old and new is by using natural materials. She is beguiled by the warmth of a jute rug, say, or vintage wicker shades that add character to a lamp. Woven materials like rattan, sculptural succulents, fossilized ammonites, and oversize pieces of smoke quartz are other examples of elements she embraces from the natural world while, from an architectural perspective, she allows external views to influence and determine the ideal floor plan.

For Berkus, the addition of botanicals to a room is instantly uplifting, which is why his spaces typically feature a bounty of greenery. Berkus blends these elements with vintage and antique furniture. This duo always finds creative solutions to address challenges such as budget or time constraints, but the integrity of the project is meaningless if it isn't deeply personal.

OPPOSITE: The casual look of the dining area of this Los Angeles residence reflects the ease of bringing the outside in as often as possible.

FOLLOWING SPREAD: California living happens outside as much as it does inside in Nate Berkus and Jeremiah Brent's former home in Los Angeles. The pool area includes a pergola with stucco banquettes, an antique stone fountain, and cement tiles from Granada Tile. A collection of ceramic Peruvian Pucara bulls displayed on the back wall personalizes the space.

ABOVE: For Nate Berkus and Jeremiah Brent's town house in New York City's West Village, the designers worked with a neutral palette and added a lot of texture like the Hjorth chest, an antique farmhouse table mounted to the wall as a console, suede club chairs, and a textured stone pot with an olive tree to create a layered look that feels elegant and livable at the same time.

OPPOSITE: The primary bedroom entry of a Seattle home features a patinated steel and marble-topped console by Rose Uniacke and a stacked plywood impression chair by Julian Mayor. The painting is by Ethan Cook.

DESIGN GUIDE

Contrasts and Curation

I have long had a penchant for blending organic shapes and textures with furniture that has either a classical or a more structured contemporary shape. The surprising synergy I discover when I mix contrasting elements energizes me. The key to managing this approach is to exercise some restraint in the layering, so that the focus is on a handful of styles and key pieces that hold meaning.

Additionally, sticking to a distinct and consistent color palette throughout the room allows you to blend furniture styles and elements from different periods more seamlessly. A fail-safe technique when experimenting with design elements from varying eras is to work with a palette of textured neutrals (black, gray, cognac, nude, cream, to name but a few). This combination often results in a space that possesses a personal and effortlessly chic quality.

Quality

Quality is at the forefront of my design choices. I prefer to work with a simple canvas filled with a few well-made things. You can always add objects at a later stage in the design process; working on spaces in phases sometimes brings more perspective, functionally and aesthetically speaking. Each area needs to be lived in and have its moments in order for you to see its full potential.

Be Curious and Take Inspiration from Everywhere

Educate your eye by reading, finding resources online, studying design masters, and visiting stores that interest you, which can help you gather your own visual library and cultivate your personal taste.

Mix old and new—vintage and antiques infuse a space with a sense of history and soul, freshness and patina.

Travel—whether near or far—not only brings all kinds of inspiration, but it also expands your frame of reference and delivers a wide canvas for endless creativity.

Adding elements from your life is key to putting together an authentic and meaningful look. Objets d'art, valued mementos of the past, favorite photographs, and coffee table books depicting wanderlust dreams or interests can help layer your space with beautiful sentiment. Surrounding yourself with these simple yet expressive accessories will bring you comfort and joy.

PAGE 188: A traditional crystal chandelier is given a naturalistic twist with the addition of raffia shades. I love the high-low mix of these materials.

OPPOSITE: A vintage classic Italian wooden table is a statement piece in my modern Manila dining room. It was refurbished by Oz Gallery in a washed finish. Above it, a copper vessel hosts kudu bones, family frames, and an antique bell from Myanmar.

I always like to add moments of lightheartedness and fun to my interiors to lend a sense of ease to a space. Examples of this include my favorite feathered Porta Romana Duck Feet Lamp and my children's framed artwork (an idea discovered in India Hicks's book *Island Style*) under our city apartment staircase. They bring effortless magic to our home and soften any formality.

Executing Your Dream Design

INSPIRING MOOD BOARDS

Similar to how I work when conceptualizing new furniture for Philux, I always start by collecting images that I am drawn to and putting together a general mood board to get the right feel for your dream space. Gathering inspiration is one of my favorite parts of the design process. Though I enjoy discovering things online, I still make sure to go through coffee table books and magazines and to visit places to stimulate my dreams.

SHOP SLOWLY

I used to be an impulsive buyer but have slowly learned to take things as they come and consider budget, form, function, and longevity before making purchases. Below are some questions to ask yourself before closing a deal: Is this piece functional? How will I use it and what role does it have in the intended space? Does this piece move me? Does it fit my budget? Can this piece be reused in a different setting over a period of time?

BUDGETS AND COLLABORATIONS

Deciding on a budget and finding the right people to work with prove key to any successful project. The design process requires careful study and pencil pushing as this enables you to work on balancing your priorities. Whether it be the general architecture and layout, interior design, lighting, styling, landscaping, or just a small refresher, all design elements must be considered and thoroughly accounted for when meeting with your team.

From our experiences, we worked closely with the architect and lighting designer (when needed) at the beginning of the project. Once we decided on the concept, we moved on to the general interiors, and then to the soft furnishings and landscape. Many of these elements can be worked on in parallel, but you should prepare your schedule, task list, and priorities systematically because a successful project demands careful timing and budgeting. Substantial resources are not required for purchasing furnishings for your home. In fact, a constrained budget can often inspire creative interior design. Make sure to source pieces—not based on their price tag—that speak to you. They will add meaning and beauty to your living spaces.

PAGE 192, CLOCKWISE FROM TOP LEFT: Textured elements in neutral tones, such as off-white feathers, upcycled kudo bones, hand-woven textiles, and a patinated bronze vase as seen here, add subtle layers of interest.

PAGE 193: The Philux Copen desk in charcoal is paired with a black-and-white chair from Nepal with delicate bone inlay. The wall is covered in Thibaut grass cloth and the drawing is a charcoal by Filipino modernist Vicente Manansala.

OPPOSITE: An antique chest from Chris's mom is used as a side table. On top are miniature bronze chairs and a vintage rattan vase.

Design: It's All in the Details

MATERIAL MIX: LAYERING TEXTURES

To me, Mother Nature continues to be the most expressive artist, and her creations among the materials I have been most drawn to in design: natural stone, live edge wood, petrified pieces, and interesting surface characteristics, all of which can blend beautifully in a modern setting with the right intention and follow-through. Nature serves as a great inspiration for my material choices.

FURNITURE LAYERING

Many Philux furniture pieces fill our home—a mix of our standard collections and some slightly more special, ones that I had the chance to customize their sizes and shapes. When moving into any home, I first carefully study what could be brought in from our previous one, simply because I always appreciate seeing elements of the past in the present. Some pieces can be used as is and we simply have to find their rightful place in the new space, while others must be repurposed to fit in.

A lovely example of this is our travertine dining table. We had invested in an Italian piece, which sported a robustly thick rectangular glass top. Given the new curved shape of our dining room, I opted to switch the glass for a solid oval travertine tabletop, a lovely combination of old and new, composed of natural materials I'm truly inspired by. When preparing a furniture layout, allow for the key pieces that anchor your space to inform where the next one should go. Trust this layering process.

PLAYING WITH COLOR

Color can define spaces: in our city apartment, we decided on an open plan and therefore our living area flows into the den. We opted to keep things bright and airy but distinguished with colors.

Start small—if you want to add color but aren't sure how, begin with diminutive, movable items such as accent furniture, throw pillows, accessories, and greenery. This will allow you to live with the hue before fully investing in a colorway.

Commit to color—if you are sure about a Pantone direction, go all out and awaken your space with a punch of color. This means committing to a scheme from the very beginning by painting a wall, adding a vibrant rug, or investing in a bold piece of furniture. Anchoring a room with color will immediately give it life; be mindful of the layering and stick to your color story throughout the design process.

Art as a color anchor—a statement art piece can inform the tones of a room by matching or complementing them. This is a foolproof way of tying

PAGE 196, CLOCKWISE FROM TOP LEFT, AND PAGE 197: Wood is a versatile material as seen in these objects from my home—carved meerkats, a *Sungka* Philippine game set, a Kelly Wearstler credenza with its smooth lacquered, layered birch plywood panels, a Philippine *Bulul* carved figure, and a porcupine quill–inspired African basket.

OPPOSITE: A bathroom at Modumela House is dressed in a graphic black-and-white wallpaper pattern. The look is elevated with a simple brass mirror and traditional sconces.

a color story together. We used this technique in our Manila living room because of our love for a large painting. It ended up being the inspiration for all the other elements such as the area rug and the upholstery.

ALLOW YOUR SPACE TO "LIVE"

Make your home comfortable and livable as imperfectly perfect as it will be. This means accepting the stains, chips, and wear and tear of the space, while still maintaining it to the best of your ability. You must learn to accept and love that life leaves its marks upon your home. Though it took me a while to accept this, I now relish remembering moments that have gone by—and my home feels more soulful as a result.

PAGE 200: Blooming artichokes in a white ceramic vase are a pleasing pop of color. The traditional white beaded African statuettes and pillows covered in a linen textured fabric are wonderful accent pieces.

PAGE 201, CLOCKWISE FROM TOP LEFT: Harmonizing textures: Oxidized bronze side tables shaped like lilies. A miniature bronze leopard. A trio of living room pillows in complementary soothing colors with tactile elements. An aged wooden pot functions as a decorative element in the curio cabinet.

OPPOSITE: The colorful baskets displayed on the wall and the painted green shelves are a clever and affordable way to add vibrance and depth to our girls' bedroom at Modumela House. A printed cloth was added to the white lampshade for a playful touch.

PAGE 204, CLOCKWISE FROM TOP LEFT: Sculptural decorative elements can come in many forms, from dried berry branches to a Chinese Tang dynasty horse to African woven-reed baskets trimmed in cowrie shells. A framed Peter Beard lion photo collage leans against the wall where many of our coffee table books are displayed.

PAGE 205: My vanity, a carved table from India, is paired with a Malawi chair. The contrasting brass mirror and standing lamp are sleek modern designs.

AT WORK

PHILUX: A FAMILY STORY

PAGE 206: Furniture and accessories in varying materials, patterns, and textures come together beautifully in this inspired dining room, curated by Philux Spaces, the brand's in-house interior design arm.

PAGE 207: Furniture woodworking jigs hang in the Philux workshop.

OPPOSITE: Through its practice of age-old Filipino craftsmanship and support of Filipino artisans, Philux works toward championing what local design, talent, and trade have to offer. What started as a husband-and-wife partnership with two carpenters has become a two-hundred-person team involved in production and retail.

My parents established Philux in 1979, focusing first on exporting locally made artifacts and, later, retailing furniture. I grew up watching them tackle the challenges of entrepreneurship, and because of that, I have always felt part of their business journey. Although our family's European and African roots inform much of our aesthetic and business philosophy, the creation of a proudly Filipino design remains the foundation of our tradition and innovative family spirit.

My mother had a very hands-on approach to the business, balancing her work responsibilities with taking care of me and my sister, Jessica. When we entered our teens, we joined her on visits to showrooms, dawdling in the stores while she zipped between meetings. I also have memories of visiting my dad's turf, a workshop in Quezon City filled with 1970s-era Italian woodworking machines manned by skilled Filipino carpenters. I remember leaving my child-sized handprints on the freshly poured cement in front of his office.

Although I didn't concentrate on design when I left to study economics and art history at Sarah Lawrence College in New York, I grasped the opportunity to work at Philux when I returned to the Philippines, after stints in Paris and London. Jessica joined us three years later, fresh from acquiring her design degree from Parsons School of Design in New York City. She has been a constant colleague and soundboard.

Philux Craft—Honing Traditional Filipino Skill

Interior designer Christiane Lemieux once said, "Quality in what we live with affects the quality of our lives and we all deserve to live beautifully," a philosophy I have embraced and internalized. I believe that you cannot overestimate the value of quality. If you can afford it, less is more. This ethos is one of the foundations of Philux. Simply put, we are passionate about doing things well. We aim to preserve Filipino craftsmanship by developing new skills and techniques, while staying open to the advantages presented by technology.

I'd like to think of Philux as the opposite of fast fashion. We are slow and meticulous, understanding that every step in the manufacturing process contributes to overall quality. Small imperfections characterize our pieces, arising from the raw materials or our traditional process.

OPPOSITE: Our Embla dining chair, a piece from the Scandiniana Collection, is one of Philux's most iconic designs. Through the gentle curvature of its solid wooden frame, the design emphasizes the natural beauty of wood, the material Philux has always honored.

ABOVE: The Pacific Collection, which is grounded in comfort, functionality, and design, maintains a luxurious aesthetic and feel with deep seating, plush pillows, solid wood tops, and metal accents. My girls are often the first to test our new designs.

Far from marring the final product, they enhance its personality and make it even more special. The end result? "Conscious luxury, crafted locally."

The Design Process

For me, collaborating in design has always been a fluid and natural process. Jess and I are both visual people and delight in translating our sources of inspiration into furniture designs or broader interior conceptions. Our sources of inspiration tend to be diverse, ranging from the mundane, as when we study our wood off-cuts (the timber we no longer use in the furniture construction process) to upcycle and integrate them into new designs, to unforgettable images we see online, from thought-provoking articles to our exhilarating travels in places such as the Swiss mountains, the Philippine islands, and the African wilderness. Whatever their source, our inspirations evoke strong emotional responses, feelings of peace or happiness, and it's from this base that we start to develop our ideas.

This process begins with the compilation of a storyboard reflecting the particular mood we wish to conjure. We then brainstorm around how and where this mood is lacking from our existing collections, so that we can introduce something a little different. We seek to launch fresh concepts every year, whether in the materials we use or in our construction techniques.

OPPOSITE, CLOCKWISE FROM TOP: The natural beauty of wood grain is manifest in the Facet dining table and Embla Abaca dining chairs, all in walnut. As we continue to source from nature and be inspired by its beauty, we make a conscious effort to utilize sustainably sourced wood as much as possible. The Palma coffee table, a part of our first foray into outdoor living. Like all Philux pieces, it is available in multiple wood and finish options, allowing the furniture selection process to be a creative and personal experience. *Solihiya*, a humble rattan weave, is a mainstay of Filipino design. Here, the weaves of the Pouf Solihiya ottoman complement those of the locally handwoven abaca rugs—a testament to the charm of natural materials.

PAGE 214: The Maxwell armoire and Stockholm bed in situ. Designs that harmoniously fuse solid wood elements with our *solihiya* accents and streamlined silhouettes.

PAGE 215: A close-up of the chevron pattern of our Copen console table in ash.

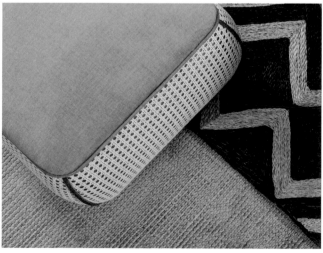

Philux Now

I like to think that furniture can play a role in culture and history. I take pride in the belief that our pieces are not only used with enjoyment but also passed on from one generation to another. We place a fresh spin on local creativity by drawing inspiration from personal memories and everyday Philippine objects like baskets, handwoven textiles, and rugs—creating a new style of timeless Filipino design with a strong international perspective. Our collaborations with designers such as Bea Valdes and brands like Louis Vuitton have allowed us to emphasize the emotive and design-led narrative of our company, while also melding distinctive idioms to create an exciting new aesthetic.

Sustainability also drives our design, as we keep our social and environmental impact in mind. Sustainability is, indeed, a journey—to which we fiercely commit as a team driving our business forward. We have implemented a multifaceted program to entrench sustainability in every aspect of the business, from production to the supply chain. Our production philosophy echoes that of Yvon Chouinard's Patagonia brand: "if it can't be reused, repaired, refurbished, refinished, resold, or recycled, then it should be restricted, removed from production, or redesigned."

We have started simply, sourcing our biggest raw material—wood—responsibly. Most of our solid wood and veneer comes from sustainable forests. We are also working to lower the impact of our single-use plastic, sending waste to an eco-hub, which upcycles the majority of retrieved plastic packaging into eco-bricks, to be used in public development projects like local schools. We constantly challenge ourselves to think of more sustainable ways to design, manufacture, and retail consciously. In this, as with everything, we are guided by the determination to leave our world a better place for future generations.

OPPOSITE: The Stockholm two-seater sofa at the workshop, where it was conceived. The Philux production standard merges beauty and durability—the very essence of fine furniture making.

LEFT: The Alva dining table, an artful twist on the classic round dining table, features a wooden tabletop set on a pedestal base with a fluted design and a brass accent. It is surrounded by matching Alva dining chairs. This ensemble is a contemporary take on mid-century modern design sensibilities.

PHOTOGRAPHY CREDITS

Dana Allen: pages 60–61, 84

Peter Anderson/Lapalala Wilderness: page 84

Paola Aseron: pages 25, 33, 35, 37, 41 (bottom), 44, 46 (bottom left), 48–49, 50, 51, 52, 53, 114–115, 118–119, 121, 191, 192 (top right, bottom left), 196 (bottom right), 201 (top left, bottom right), 204 (top left, top right)

Rolly Bayarang: page 156

EJ Bonagua: page 164

Malcom Brown: pages 174, 176, 177

Kenneth Cobonpue: page 167

Roger Davies: page 183

Christopher Dibble: pages 184–85, 187

Nicole Franzen: page 186

Courtesy of GLOW (Festival of Lights): pages 160–61

Brittan Goetz: pages 9, 181

Francisco Guerrero: pages 2, 18, 20–21, 23, 28–29, 31, 32, 38–39, 40, 41 (top), 42–43, 45, 46 (top left and right, bottom right), 47, 54–55, 56, 57, 108, 111, 112–113, 120, 189, 193, 195, 197, 204 (bottom left)

Rio Helmi: page 172

India Hicks: pages 179, 180

Micky Hoyle: page 11

Veronica Kotze: pages 154–55

Personal photographic collection: pages 13, 15, 16, 19, 159

Stephano Scata: page 169

Lionel Smit: page 153

Denison Tan: pages 22, 165, 206, 210, 211, 213, 214, 215, 218–219

Meilin Tan: page 163

Tarzeer Pictures: pages 207, 209, 217

Alina Vlasova: pages 170, 171, 173

Elsa Young: pages 5, 6, 26, 58, 59, 63, 64–65, 66, 68, 70, 71, 72–73, 74, 75, 76–77, 78, 79, 80–81, 82–83, 85, 86–87, 88–89, 90, 91, 92–93, 94, 95, 96–97, 98, 99, 100, 101, 102, 103, 104–105, 106, 107, 109, 116, 117, 123, 124, 125, 126, 127, 128–129, 130, 131, 132–133, 134, 135, 136, 137, 138, 139, 140, 141,142–143, 145, 146, 147, 149, 150–151, 188, 192 (top left, bottom right), 196 (top left, top right, bottom left), 199, 200, 201 (top right, bottom left), 202, 204 (bottom right), 205, 221, 223

Chris Yuhico: page 159

CAPTIONS

ABOVE: For our Lapalala home, we strived to utilize local materials. The vibrant rust-hued stone seen throughout was excavated from the rock hill behind the house. The lath ceilings lend a traditional African touch, while the colors of the walls mimic those found in nature. The shaded poolside porch at the end of the lawn is our preferred spot for enjoying the outdoors—midday to soak up some sun and in the evenings surrounded by the glow of lanterns.

PAGE 2: The dining room of our Manila home is all about beige, cream, and brown tones. A vintage 1950s Pierre Jeanneret chair from Chandigarh is paired with Kelly Wearstler's Trancas credenza. The wooden vessels by Industria and the delicate rock-crystal sconces by Phoenix Gallery, New York, flank an oil painting by Fernando Zóbel de Ayala y Montojo, and add dark contrasting accents.

PAGE 5: A family portrait—I'm seated on our Modumela House lawn with my husband, Chris, and our daughters, Andrea and Arielle.

PAGE 6: Modumela House greets visitors with earthy textures, such as a lath ceiling, cladded sandstone, and woven African textiles. Opposite the rustic antique wooden door is a picture window with a magnificent view of the bush.

ACKNOWLEDGMENTS

The first person I would like to thank is my husband, Chris, whose love and encouragement from day one have allowed *Embracing Natural Design* to become a reality. The homes and life we have built together provide my foundation. You have been a steadfast and treasured partner throughout this journey, and I cannot thank you enough.

To my daughters, Andrea, Arielle, and little Anouck on the way, who have given me the gift of motherhood and who inspire me every day.

To my parents, Max and Zelda, for always cheering me on and my sister, Jessica, for her invaluable insight.

I am so appreciative of the brilliant and talented team who worked with me to bring this book to life: my editor, Sandy Gilbert Freidus, for reading my very first email and for believing in me; my publishing consultant, Ingeborg Pelser, for patiently guiding me through this novel process; and my book designer, Marius Roux, for your beautiful creative input. Thank you three for enduring the New York, Cape Town, Manila time zones—a true transcontinental collaboration.

To my publisher, Rizzoli, and Charles Miers for supporting my vision. To photographers Elsa Young, Francisco Guerrero, and Paola Aseron for creating magic through your lenses, and to my friend Stephanie Zubiri for making sure the book stayed true to my voice.

I am grateful to the contributors who have been a great source of inspiration to me. Thank you for generously participating in this project; it is an honor to include you in my book: to India Hicks for your endorsement and kind words, Yvonne O'Brien, Tim Steyn, Lionel Smit, Fernando Zóbel de Ayala, Olivia d'Aboville, Bea Valdes, Marga Valdes Trinidad, Kenneth Cobonpue, Elora Hardy, Hadley Wiggins-Marin, Nate Berkus, and Lauren Buxbaum Gordon.

To my Philux team. I am thankful to be working with you on championing Filipino craft and design.

And lastly to my family, friends, and readers whose support warms my heart.

STEPHANIE KIENLE GONZALEZ is at the helm of Philux, her family's Philippine-based lifestyle brand that champions Filipino design. One of Philux's projects is the design of Louis Vuitton's Manila flagship store. Stephanie also co-hosts *Metro Home*, the award-winning Philippine lifestyle show, and she has received press in such publications as *Town & Country* and *Philippine Tatler*. Stephanie serves as an advocate for conservation on the World Wildlife Fund's Next Generation Council and is on the board of trustees of Habitat for Humanity Philippines.

Philux.ph and stephaniekienlegonzalez.com.

Designer and author INDIA HICKS is known for her chic laid-back style.

First published in the United States of America in 2022 by
Rizzoli International Publications, Inc.
300 Park Avenue South
New York, NY 10010
www.rizzoliusa.com

© 2022 Stephanie Kienle Gonzalez
Foreword by India Hicks

Publisher: Charles Miers
Editor: Sandra Gilbert Freidus
Editorial Coordination: Ingeborg Pelser
Assistant Writer: Lisa Witepski
Editorial Assistance: Hilary Ney, Kelli Rae Patton, Rachel Selekman
Art Direction and Design: Marius Roux, MR Design
Design Assistance: Olivia Russin
Production Manager: Kaija Markoe
Managing Editor: Lynn Scrabis

Printed in China

2022 2023 2024 2025 / 10 9 8 7 6 5 4 3 2 1

ISBN: 978-0-8478-7155-1
Library of Congress Control Number: 2021948770

Visit us online:
Facebook.com/RizzoliNewYork
instagram.com/rizzolibooks
twitter.com/Rizzoli_Books
pinterest.com/rizzolibooks
youtube.com/user/RizzoliNY
issuu.com/Rizzoli